PRIVATE LESSONS

by
Jean Marc Belkadi

ISBN 978-0-634-02760-6

HAL•LEONARD®
CORPORATION
7777 W. BLUEMOUND RD. P.O. BOX 13819 MILWAUKEE, WI 53213

In Australia Contact:
Hal Leonard Australia Pty. Ltd.
22 Taunton Drive   P.O. Box 5130
Cheltenham East, 3192   Victoria, Australia
Email: ausadmin@halleonard.com

Visit Hal Leonard Online at
www.halleonard.com

Table of Contents

	Page	CD Track

Introduction

Though the birth of tapping is largely associated with the eighties decade, players had begun experimenting with it as early as the mid-to-late seventies. Namely among them are session whiz Larry Carlton and the inimitable Jeff Beck. It was only a matter of time before someone would truly exploit the technique and harness the potential it possessed. Eddie Van Halen almost single-handedly introduced the technique to the guitar world with the release of *Van Halen* near the turn of the decade. Rock guitar players everywhere jumped on the bandwagon, and within a few years a new breed of tappers emerged with their own style. Players such as Greg Howe, Steve Lynch, Reb Beach, and Jennifer Batten twisted and reinvented the technique, achieving unprecedented results.

More recently in the nineties, fusion and contemporary guitarists Stanley Jordan and T.J. Helmerich took it to the next level, in many instances getting rid of the pick all together.

The objective of this book is to provide some different ways of using the tapping technique. The licks presented here draw from the styles of all the above-mentioned masters. Therefore, a great variety of techniques will be covered. It is hoped that you'll find many ideas in this book that you'll be able to incorporate into your own playing. Good luck and enjoy.

About the Audio

Throughout this book, the numbers below the audio symbols (Track 1) indicate the CD track number where each example will be found on the accompanying CD.

Each example is played at full tempo, and most are repeated at half speed. In addition, short introductory phrases (which are not transcribed in the examples) are sometimes included to provide a better sense of context and to maintain an improvisational feel.

Chapter One
BLUES AND CLASSIC TAPPING LICKS

In this chapter we'll take a look at some spins on tapping classics. We'll be incorporating tapped bends, pedal points, and open strings, among other devices.

We'll start off with a well-known tapping lick in Ami. This one takes place entirely on the B string, outlining several triads, including Ami, F, and B°.

Track 1

Here's a similar lick in Emi that makes use of the open B string as well.

Track 2

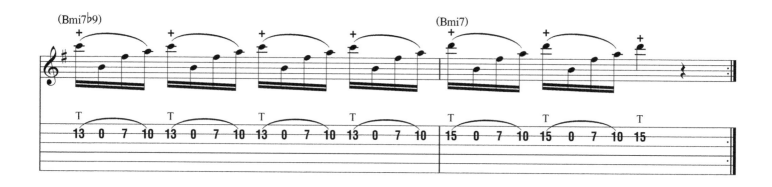

This bluesy lick in B♭ makes use of the tapped bend technique. After hammering onto the A♭ and bending up a whole step, tap onto the thirteenth fret to sound the D note, pull off to the ninth fret, and release the bend.

Track 3

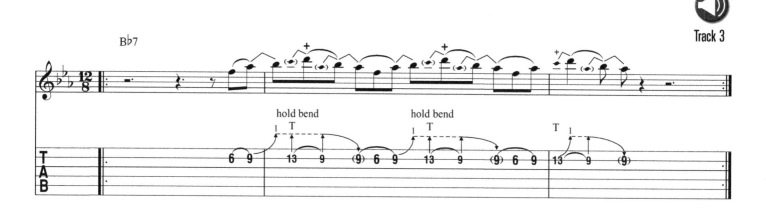

Here's a bluesy lick in A that makes use of an interesting rhythmic device. Notice that a pattern of four notes is repeated in a sextuplet rhythm, creating an offsetting effect that takes six beats to cycle back around.

Track 4

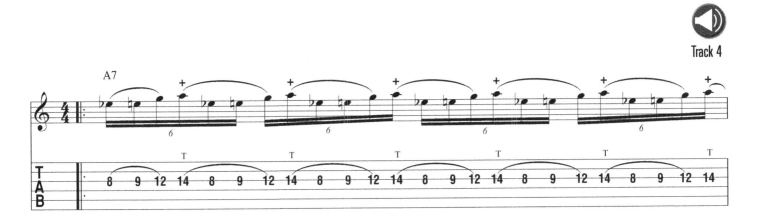

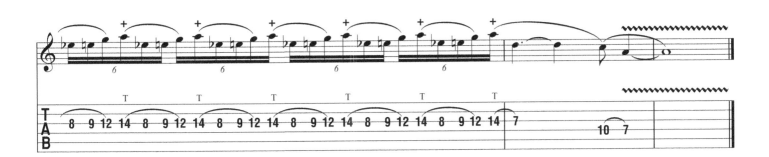

Here's an outside lick over an E7 chord that again makes use of four notes per string.

Track 5

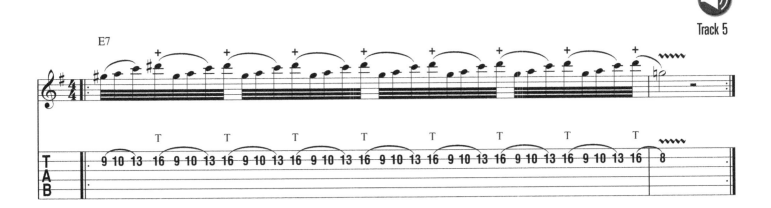

This is an interesting pedal point lick over a groove in E. Keep your left-hand index finger on the E string while hammering onto the B and G strings with your second and third fingers. Practice this idea slowly to develop rhythmic consistency.

Track 6

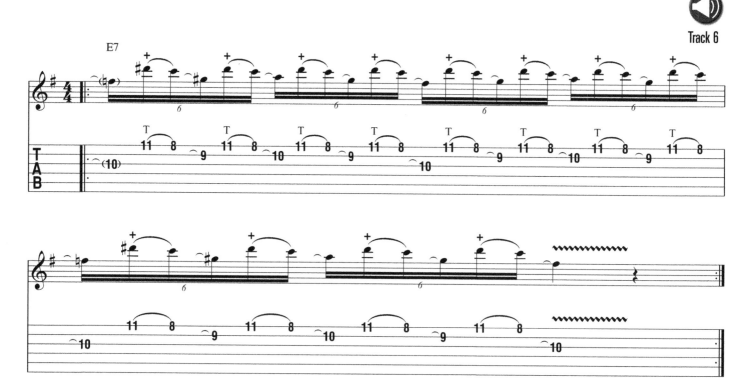

Here's a nice, fast bluesy lick over G7 that makes use of a tapped slide. Tap the B note with your right-hand index finger and then slide it up to C and back down to B before pulling it off. Try transposing this lick to your favorite key.

Track 7

This lick, also in G, uses a tapped trill. You can also try this one by tapping with the side of your pick.

Track 8

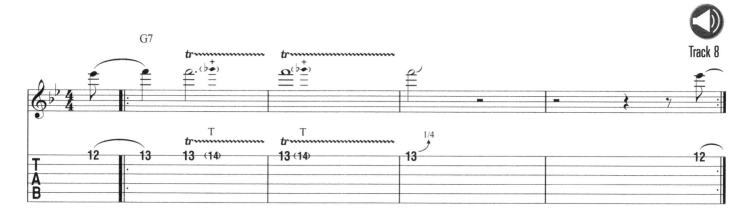

Here's a bluesy lick in Ami that makes use of two different tapped bends.

Track 9

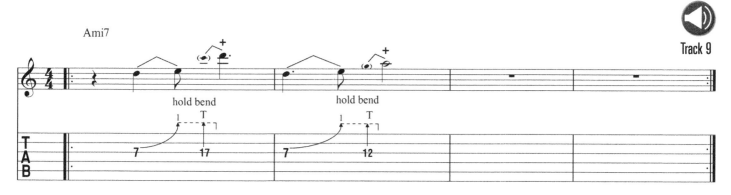

This is an interesting lick making use of a chromatic slide with the tap finger on each string.

Track 10

Here's a roller coaster pedal point lick over Emi7. Again, notice that the right-hand index finger remains on the E string the entire lick while the other left-hand fingers hammer on notes from the E blues scale.

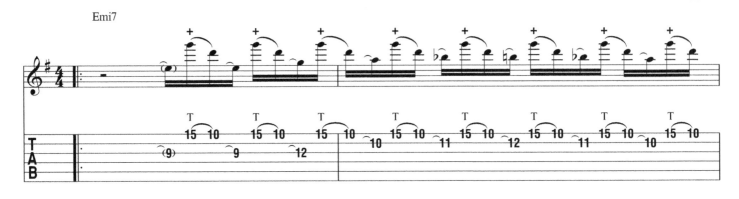

Track 11

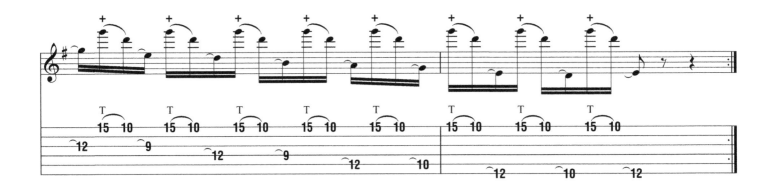

This example in Ami makes use of a tapped harmonic. After sounding the C note, quickly tap the string directly above the seventeenth fret. Release your finger as soon as you tap the string in order to

Track 12

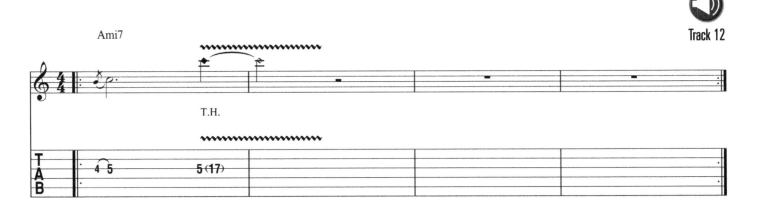

Here's a fast, repetitive blues lick in B♭ that makes use of a tapped slide and takes place entirely on the high E string.

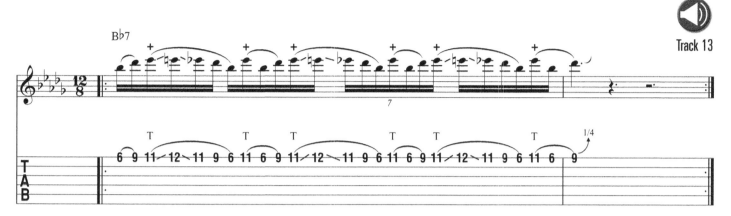

This lick makes use of the A Mixolydian mode, quickly tapping across the top three strings.

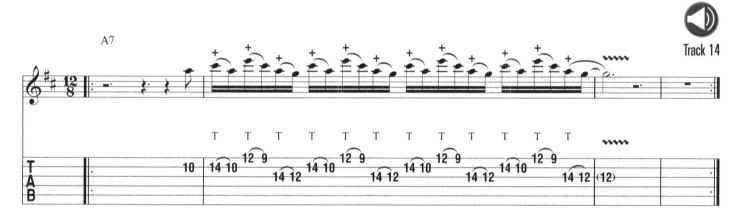

Over an E7(♭9) chord, here's a diminished sounding lick entirely on the B string.

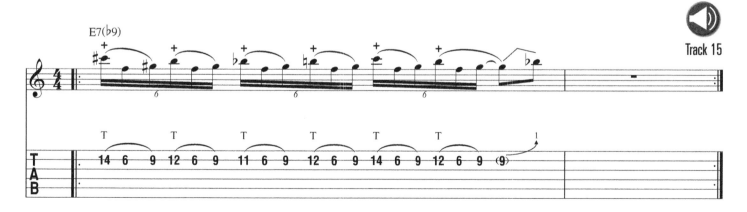

Chapter Two
SCALAR TAPPING LICKS

2

In this chapter we'll be using the tapping technique to rip through scale patterns and sequences. Here we'll see quite a bit of the left-hand "hammer-on-from-nowhere" technique. Take some extra time to make sure you're getting this clean and that the hammered-on note is clearly audible.

Here's a fast sextuplet lick in G minor that makes use of a tapped slide on the high E string.

Track 16

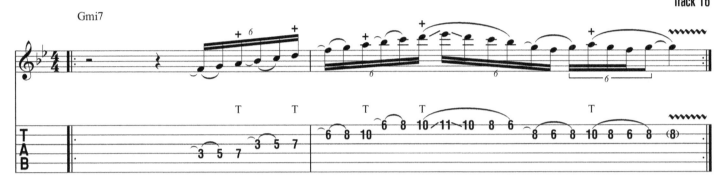

This is another sextuplet lick in G minor that ascends through all six strings. Notice the tapped chromatic C♯ passing tone in beat 3; this lends a bluesy touch to the lick.

Track 17

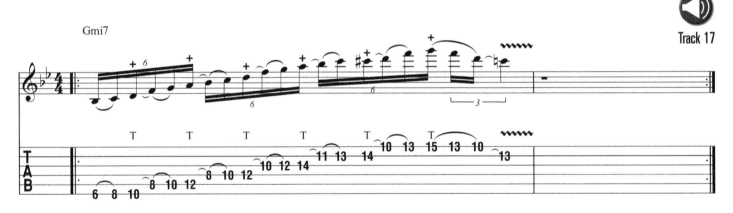

Here's an example in A minor that takes place entirely on the top two strings. The A Dorian mode is used here.

Track 18

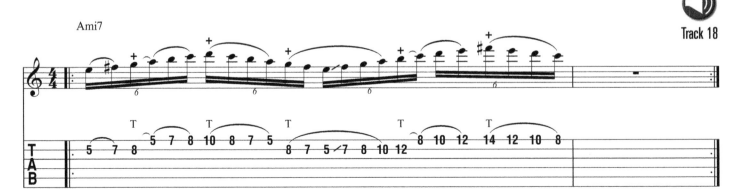

12

This lick makes a great exercise for practicing the A Dorian mode using only one string. In this case, a three-note sequence is shifted all the way up the high E string. This idea also helps us to see the scale in a horizontal fashion as opposed to the more common vertical approach.

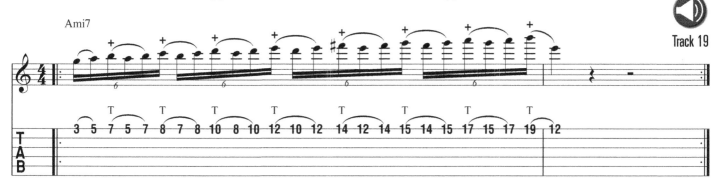

Track 19

Here's an ascending A major pentatonic (or F♯ minor pentatonic) example that uses three notes per string with a repeated note at each string cross. The sixteenth-note rhythm provides an interesting three-over-four rhythm effect here.

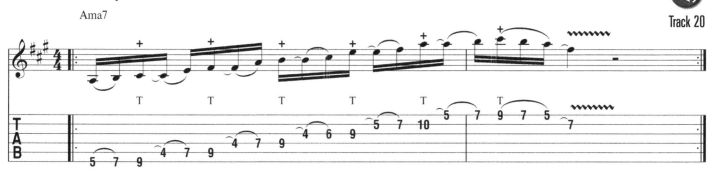

Track 20

This idea in A major mixes up notes from the A major scale on the high E and B strings for a unique sound. Try applying this pattern to other areas of the neck using the A major scale.

Track 21

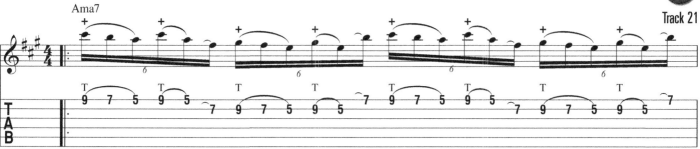

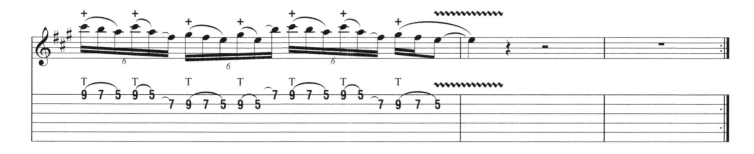

Here's a slippery lick in D Dorian that makes extensive use of slides on the high E string. This is also a great exercise with which to work on timing. This type of idea can easily be moved around the neck as well.

Track 22

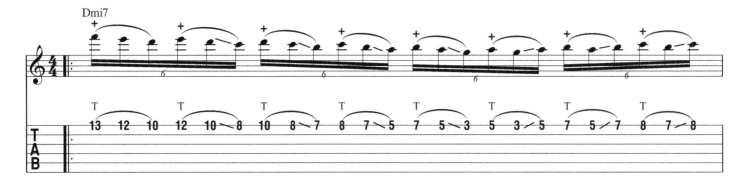

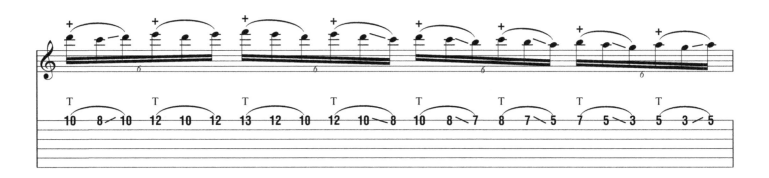

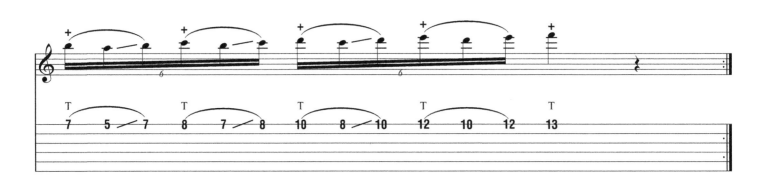

This example, also in D Dorian, takes place all within the range of a 4th on the high E string. Tapping within such close proximity of the fret hand is a great way to play more traditional sounding licks with great speed.

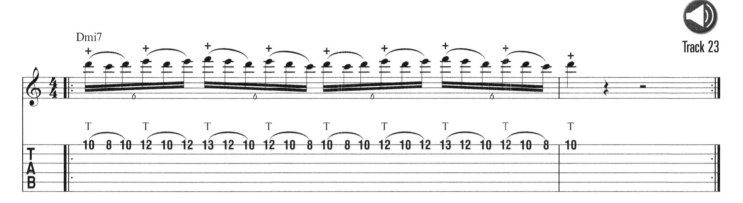

Track 23

Here's an ascending Mixolydian scale over F7 in sextuplets. Again, make sure the left-hand hammer-ons are clear.

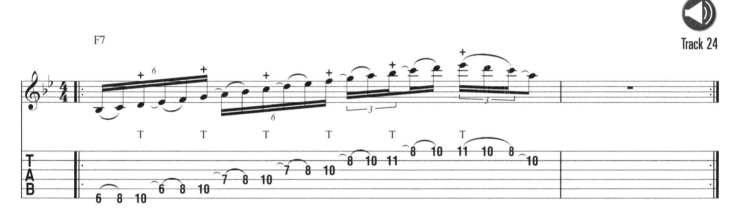

Track 24

Here's a descending version of the previous example. It's not the complete opposite, as the notes still ascend on each string.

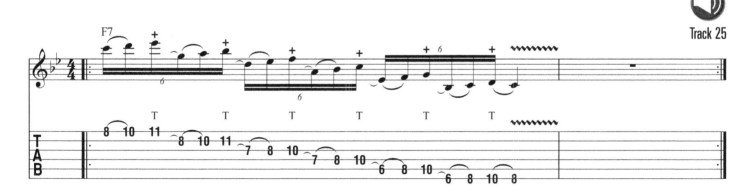

Track 25

This example sequences a pattern down the strings using the E minor pentatonic scale. Notice how you're tapping on only the twelfth fret throughout.

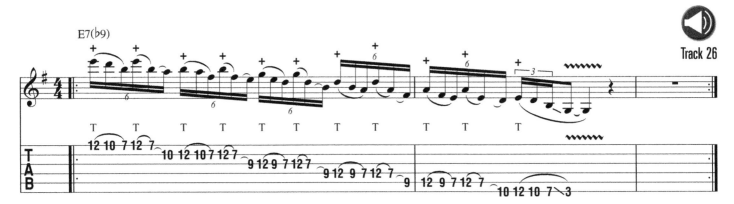

Track 26

This lick demonstrates how you can move an E minor scale fragment chromatically to create an outside sound. You can really stretch this type of thing for as long as you'd like; just make sure you come back to the key at the end.

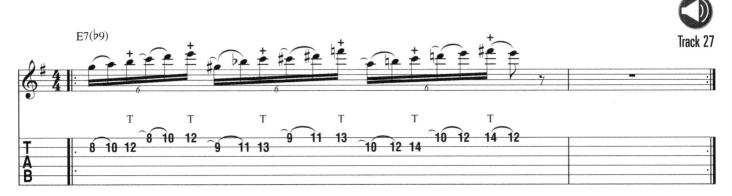

Track 27

Here's an ascending lick from the C minor pentatonic scale that makes use of three notes per string. The G string is completely skipped in this example. Even though this one is a bit tricky, this technique will be adaptable to many other licks once it's mastered.

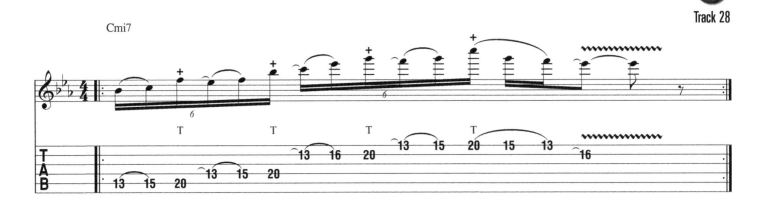

Track 28

This descending lick combines C Dorian with C minor pentatonic. Your tapping finger will move in more of a linear fashion here as well as vertically.

Track 29

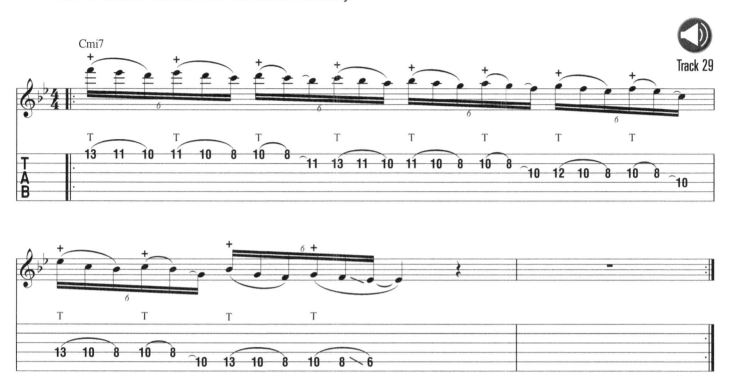

Here's a great two-octave lick that ascends with four notes per string through a combination of the E harmonic minor and natural minor scales. Since you're only tapping five notes throughout this entire example, your left hand will be forced to do most of the work here.

Track 30

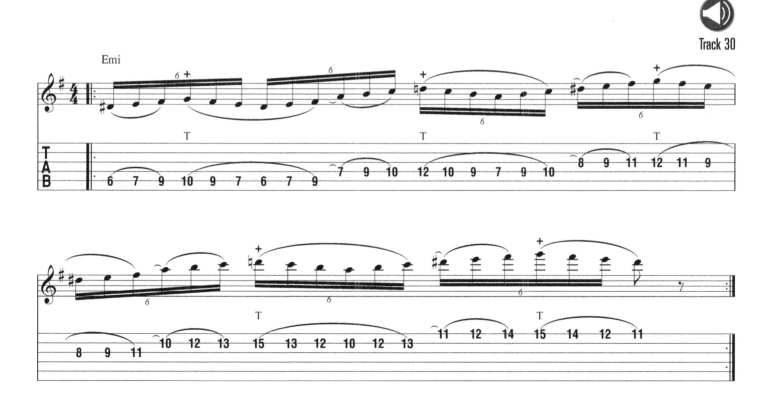

Chapter Three
TRIADS AND ARPEGGIOS

3

We're going to be applying the technique in this chapter to triads and other arpeggios. This is something for which the tapping technique is really custom made. Other than a bit of stretching in the left hand, flying through arpeggios with tapping is a breeze.

This first example moves a two-note major triad shape chromatically up two frets and back down before finishing off with a bluesy quarter-step bend. You'll be hammering onto the B string with your left-hand second finger here, so take it slowly at first and make sure you're getting this clean.

Track 31

Here's an example that moves through four triads—Ami, F, G, and Emi—with a two-string shape. Again, the second finger of your left hand is performing the hammer-ons here.

Track 32

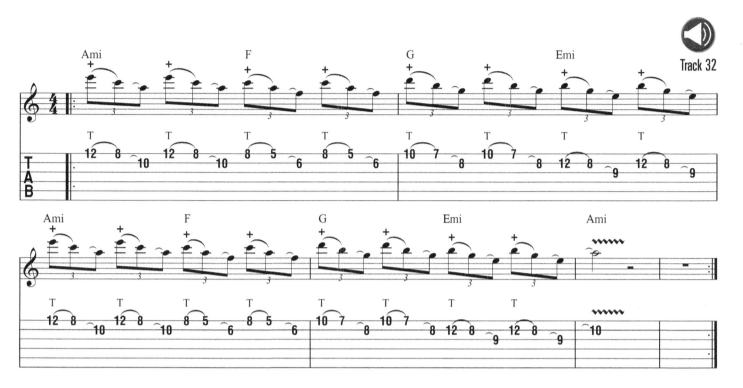

This is a B♭ augmented triad played on four strings. You can use this lick over B♭, D, or F♯ altered chords. You'll need to start this lick with your left-hand second finger. Then alternate every string between your first and second for the left-hand hammer-ons.

Track 33

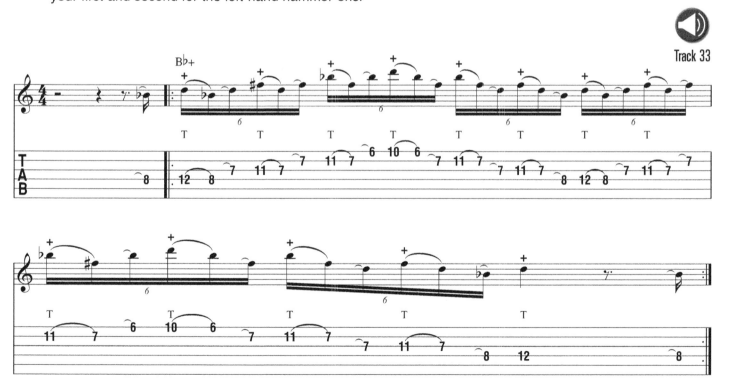

Here's an F major triad played through the top four strings. You'll need to use several different left-hand fingers for the hammer-ons here in order to make this seamless.

Track 34

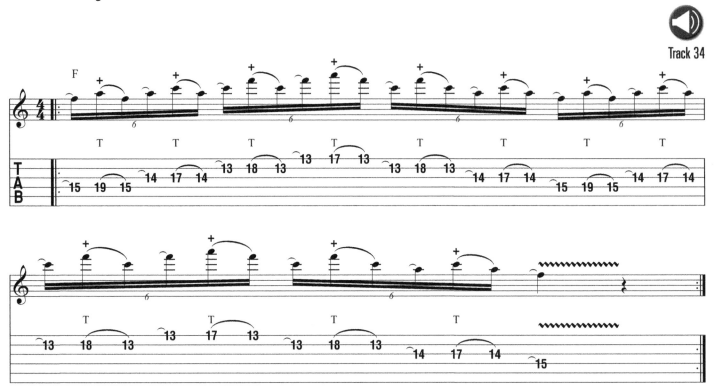

This example ascends through an A minor arpeggio almost three octaves, reaching the 7th (G) on the fifteenth fret of the high E string. You'll have to stretch a little bit in the left hand in beat 2 here.

Track 35

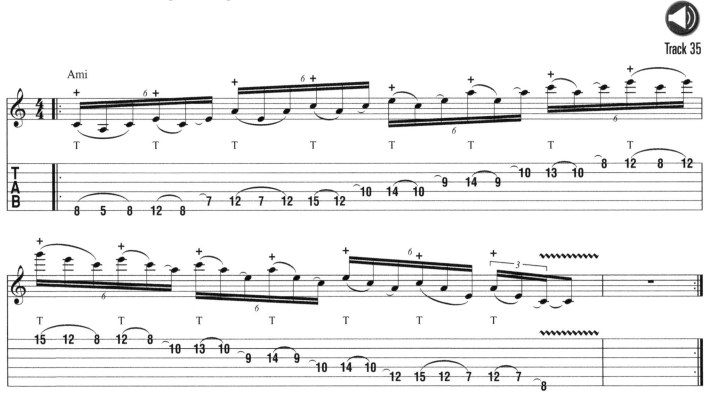

This example taps through a string skipping pattern to outline F, C, and B♭ triads. Notice that the B♭ pattern is the same as the C pattern, just transposed down a whole step. This one will take a bit of time to work up to speed.

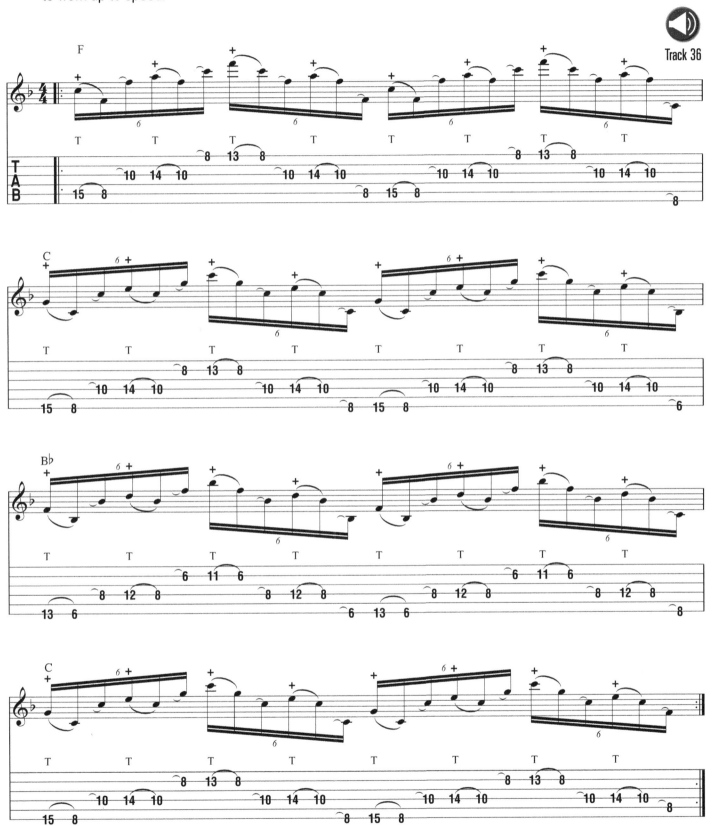

Here's an ascending F diminished arpeggio using more string skipping. In this particular example, you could use the index and middle fingers of your tapping hand if it's easier.

Track 37

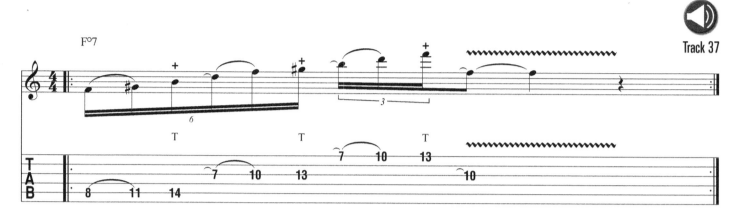

Here we see a Cma7 arpeggio lick that spans a full three octaves through all six strings. The tap is used very sparingly here.

Track 38

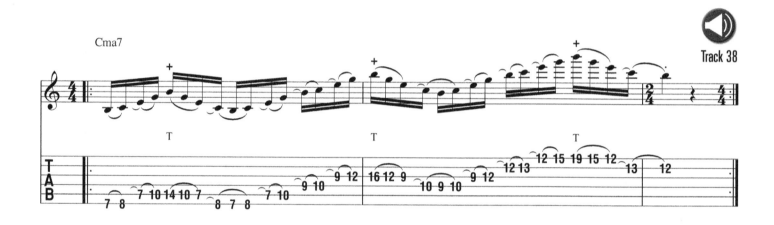

This example uses the first and second fingers of the right hand to outline a progression of C to B♭6/9. Tap the notes on the G string with your second finger and use the first finger for the notes on the low E string.

Track 39

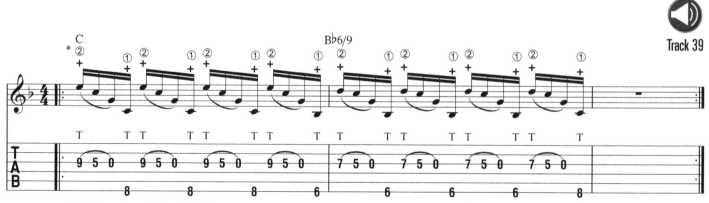

*Circled numbers indicate R.H. fingers.

In this lick, every note is either hammered on or tapped; there are no pull-offs in the entire lick. While the left hand hammers power chords, the right hand taps a G/B♭ dyad to create the harmonies of Cmi7 (no 3rd) and A♭ma9.

Track 40

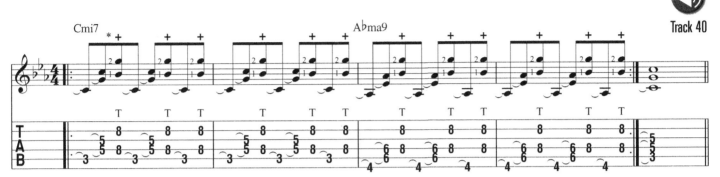

*Numbers in notation indicate R.H. fingers.

Here we're combining sweep picking, slides, string skipping, and a single tap on the high B♭ to whip through a three-octave C7 arpeggio. Since you're using your pick for this lick, you'll probably need to tap the B♭ with your middle finger.

Track 41

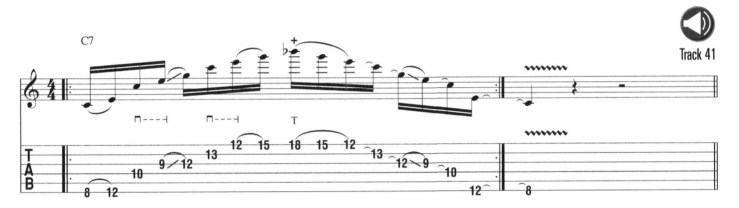

Here's a similar idea built off the fifth string that outlines an Fmi9 arpeggio. Notice that the 9th (G) is only heard once at the very peak of the lick. This helps to accentuate the extended sound.

Track 42

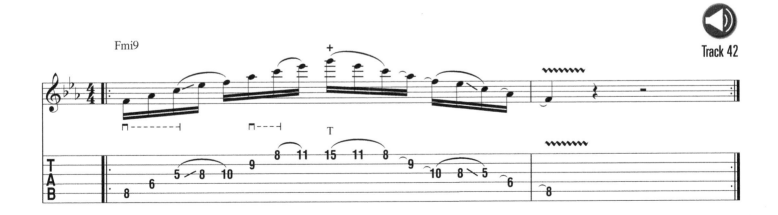

This lick blazes through a C°7 arpeggio by combining a three-note-per-string pattern with string skipping. Try alternating between your first and second fingers on the right hand for the taps in this one.

Track 43

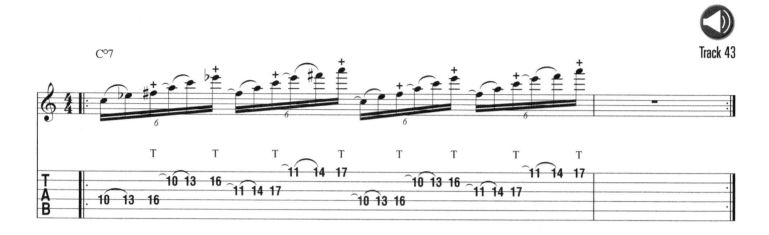

In this example, the tap is used on the high F note, while the left hand hammers on power chords below. The harmonies created here are F5, E♭sus2, and Dmi. Make sure that you're maintaining rhythmic accuracy throughout.

Track 44

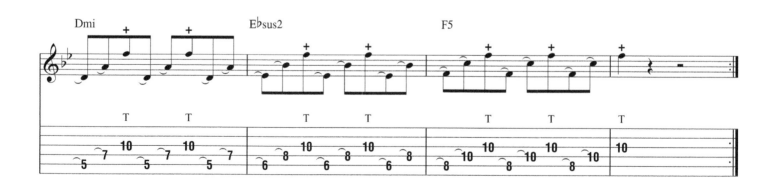

In a similar vein, left-hand octaves are hammered here, while a common E/G dyad is tapped above with the first and second fingers of the right hand. Try applying this type of idea to some of your other favorite chord progressions.

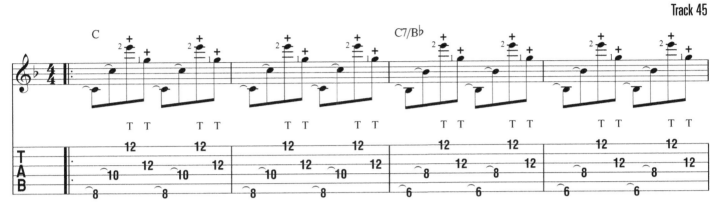

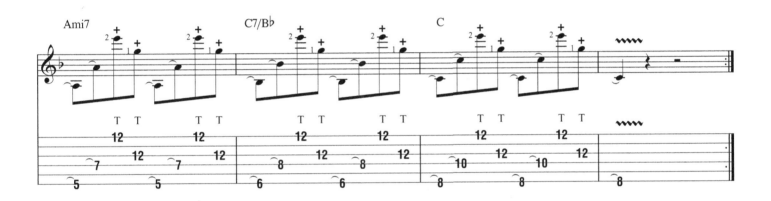

Chapter Four
4 ADVANCED TAPPING TECHNIQUES

In this chapter we'll be dealing with some more advanced tapping styles. Many of these will make use of the multi-fingered approach on the tapping hand, so if you haven't dealt much with this, some of these may take a little longer to work up.

Our first example uses a three-note pattern to ascend through an A minor pentatonic lick by way of string skipping. You're going to be using the middle and ring fingers on your right hand for this one. This will prevent you from having to jump all around with one finger. If it feels uncomfortable to use your middle and ring fingers, you can try other combinations, such as your index and ring or index and middle, until you find something that works for you.

Track 46

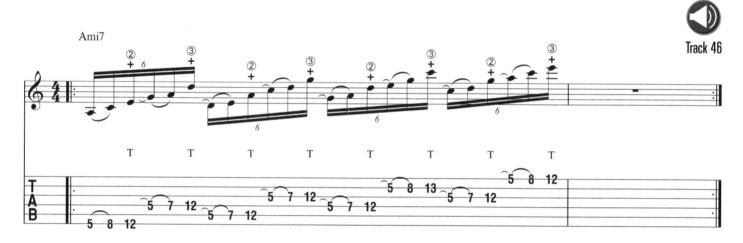

This example ascends through a C Dorian mode by using a three-note pattern consisting of two left-hand notes and one tapped note.

Track 47

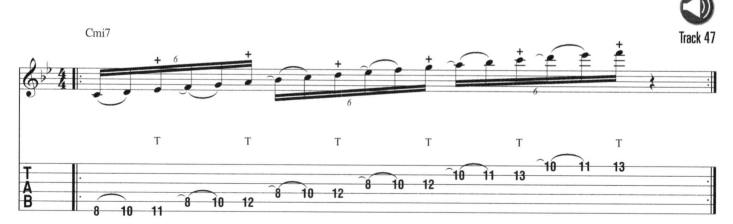

In this E minor pentatonic lick, we're skipping strings on the way up and descending straight through on the way down. Take some time working this one up to tempo.

Track 48

This is a chordal tapping lick using B♭ and A♭ power chords in the left hand and a mixture of 7ths, 6ths, and 4ths in the right hand. Notice that all of the tapped notes are derived from the B♭ major pentatonic scale. Be careful with the odd meter in this one!

Track 49

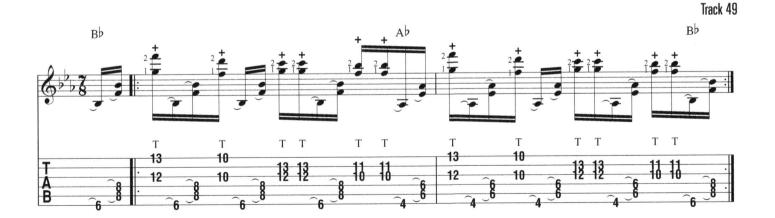

Here's a nice technique that you can use to embellish a standard chord progression. Here, taps on the twelfth fret are used to spice up standard C, Ami, and G barre chord forms.

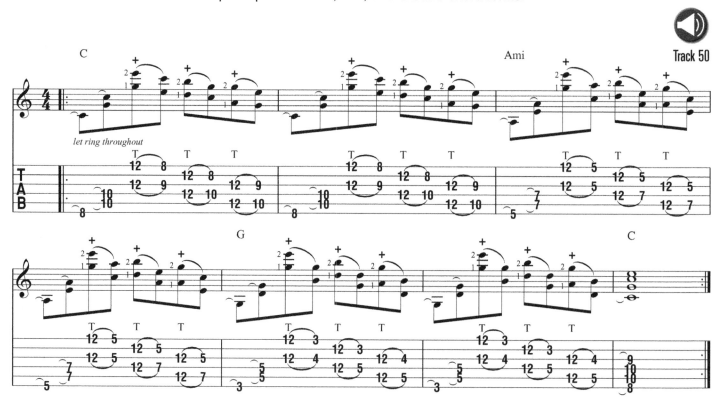

This lick demonstrates a great way to tap through a progression of arpeggios that share many common tones. Here we're using the first and second fingers of the right hand combined with string skipping to outline a progression of Emi–Emi(ma7)–Emi7–Emi6.

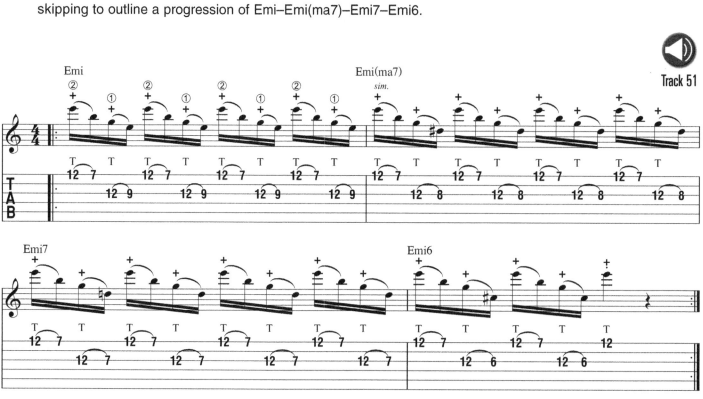

Here's another nice way to embellish a static minor chord. This example colors the Dmi7 chord with harmonized 10ths and ends with a tapped double stop at the thirteenth fret.

Track 52

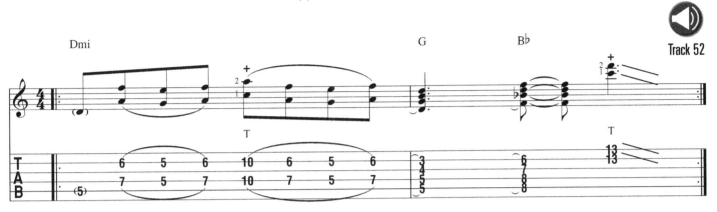

This example is hammering on D and B♭ power chords in the left hand while tapping 4ths and 3rds in the right hand derived from the D minor pentatonic scale. The rhythm here is similar to track 49, except here we're in standard 4/4 meter.

Track 53

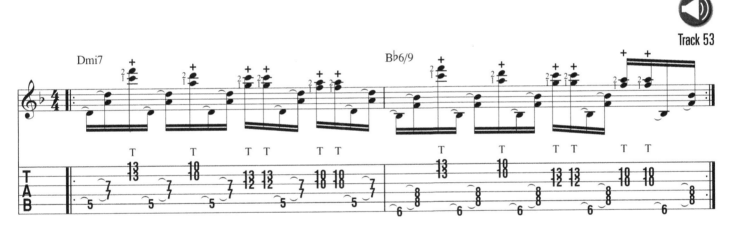

Here's an interesting example that uses double stops in both hands to embellish an A7 harmony. Start slowly with this one to make sure you're getting an accurate synchronization.

Track 54

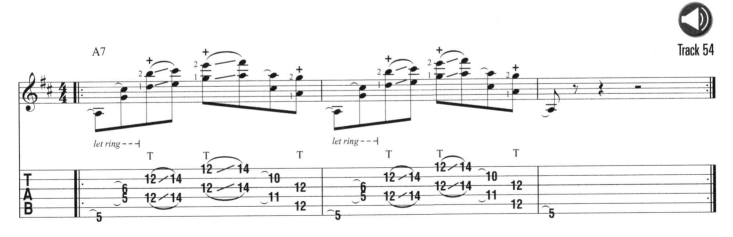

Here's a different technique. In this lick, we're barring the fifth fret with our *right-hand* first finger and hammering and pulling off above with our left hand. The notes here are derived from the A minor pentatonic scale. Try this technique with other scales.

Track 55

*Barre across 5th fret with R.H. first finger.

This is a diminished chord shape played with the two-handed chordal technique. This particular example is moving chromatically up and down. All notes here are either hammered or tapped; there are no pull-offs.

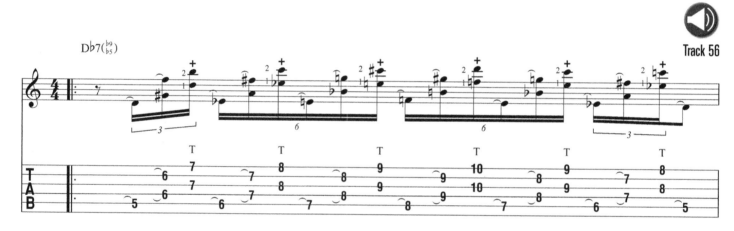

Track 56

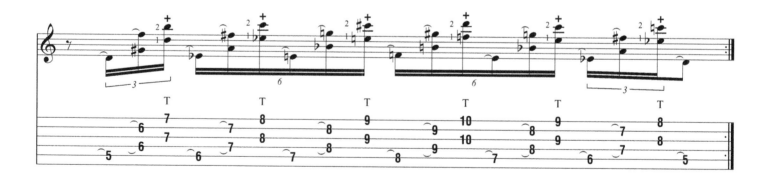

This is the same as the previous example, except here the shape is moving by minor 3rds. This may take a bit longer to work up to tempo, so start slowly to make sure you're getting it clean.

Track 57

Here's a classic jazz chord progression played with a multi-fingered approach in the right hand (three fingers) in the style of Stanley Jordan. In this style, the left hand hammers all the chords, while the right hand taps the melody above.

Track 58

*All downstemmed notes hammered on by L.H.

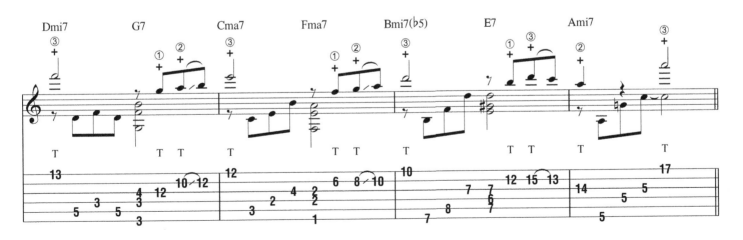

This example applies the tapping technique to a Latin feel, outlining an Ami7–D7–Gmi7–C7 progression. You may want to work the two hands up separately before putting them together.

Track 59

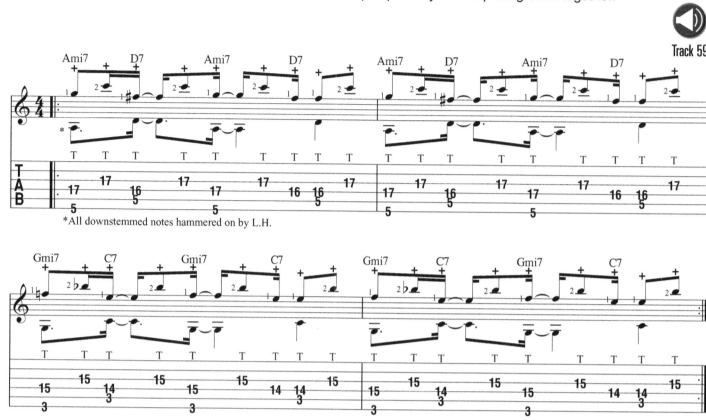

*All downstemmed notes hammered on by L.H.

Here's a cool way to play major and minor triads with tapping. Again notice how the left hand plays power chords while the right hand plays 10ths.

Track 60

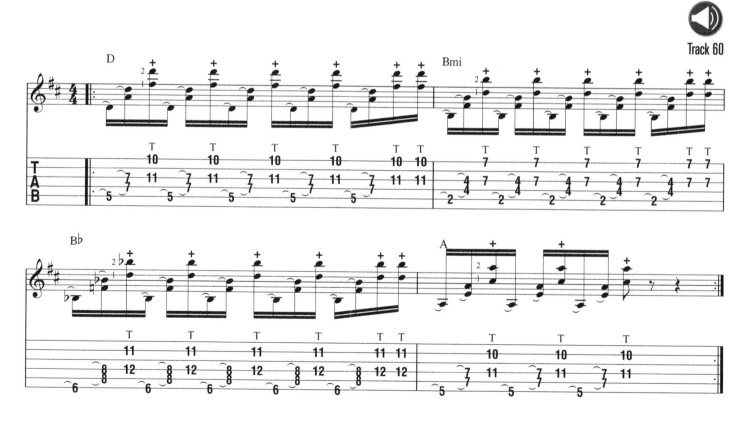

Here we see an ascending G half-whole diminished scale using four notes per string. As this is a symmetrical scale pattern, this one is fairly easy to work up to speed.

Track 61

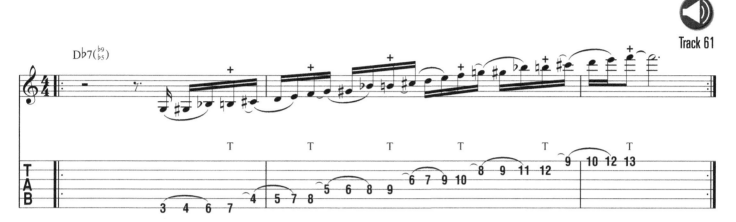

In this lick, the left hand is using notes from A Dorian, while the right hand is tapping down a C# minor pentatonic scale. The result has a nice bluesy A7 sound.

Track 62

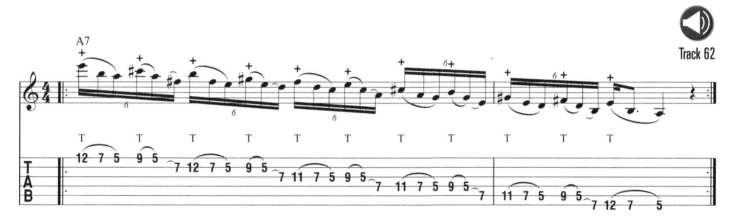

Here's another diminished example moving up in minor 3rds. Notice that, on the B string, you're hammering onto the same note with the left hand immediately after tapping it with the right hand. Practice this slowly to make sure the left-hand hammer is clearly audible.

Track 63

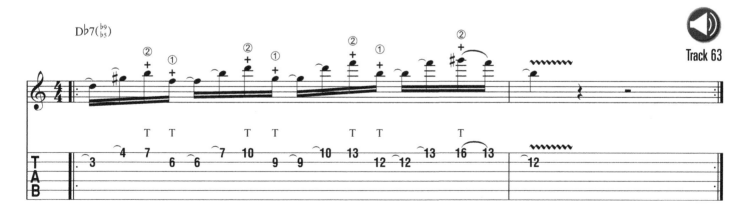

This example moves an arpeggiated diminished 7th chord chromatically. The first two notes of each shape are hammered by the left hand, while the second two are tapped by the first and second fingers of the right hand.

Track 64

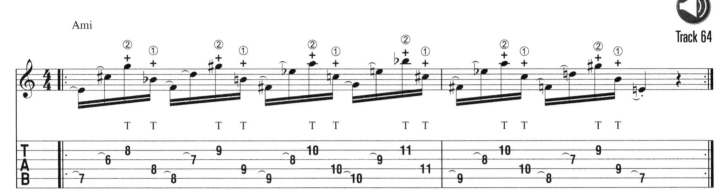

Here's an interesting way to tap through some chord inversions. In this example, the tapped note is actually lower in pitch than the left-hand notes. The chords outlined here are Cmi, G, B♭2, and C7.

Track 65

Here's another string skipping diminished pattern that's moved up chromatically. This one is a bit tricky, so start slowly and gradually build up to speed.

Track 66

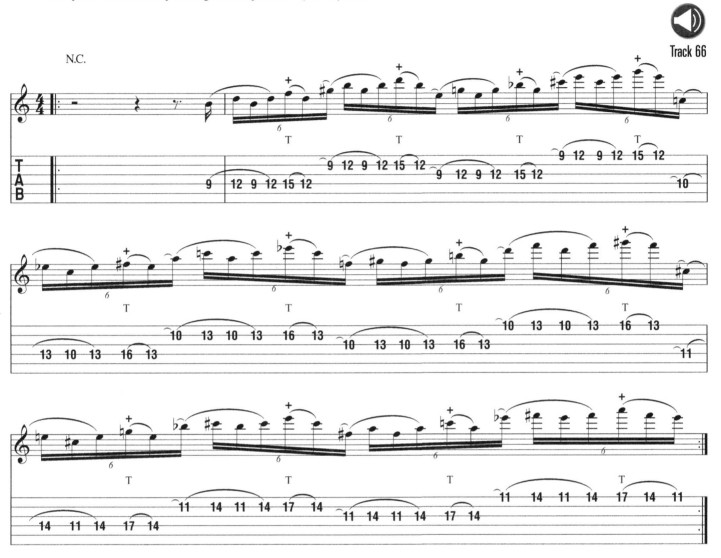

This example ascends up through an A minor pentatonic scale, including the 9th (B) at the very top. The rhythm here is especially difficult, as you're not tapping on strong beats. Start slowly and make sure you're accenting the first note of each triplet.

Track 67

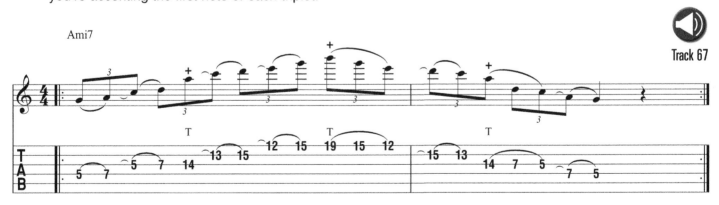

This is an interesting lick to use over a G13 harmony. You'll have to be quick with your tapping hand to pull this one off smoothly.

Track 68

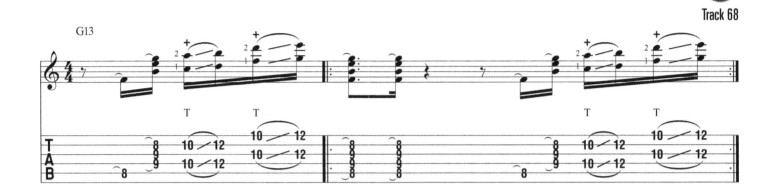

Here's a way to tap through a blues progression. Your left hand is hammering 5ths here, while your right hand is tapping a 3rd/♭7th double stop for each chord. Try this for a minor blues as well.

Track 69

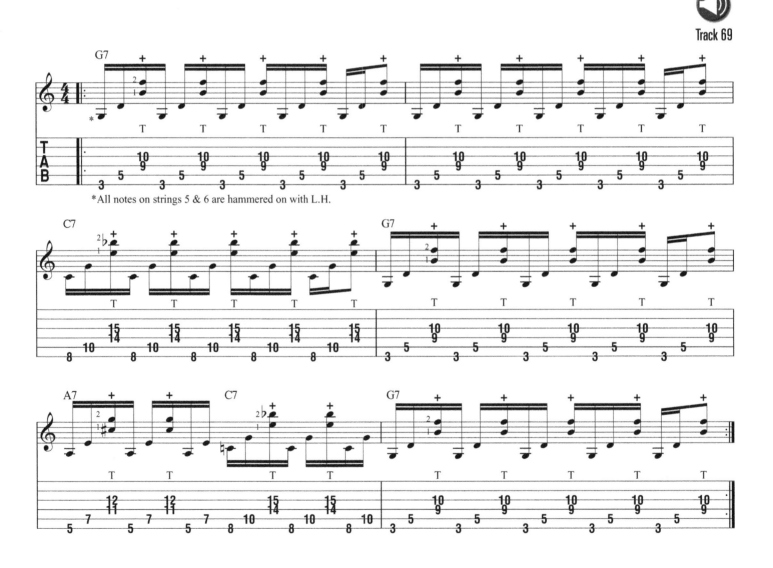

*All notes on strings 5 & 6 are hammered on with L.H.

This example uses a high tapped D pedal tone over a Cma7–Dmi7–Emi7 progression hammered out by the left hand.

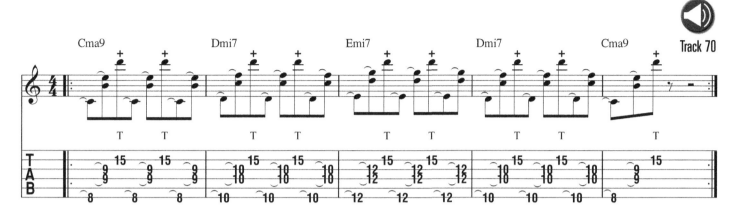

Here's a wild way to tap through a C major triad in two octaves using string skipping. Make sure the notes are even in tempo and volume.

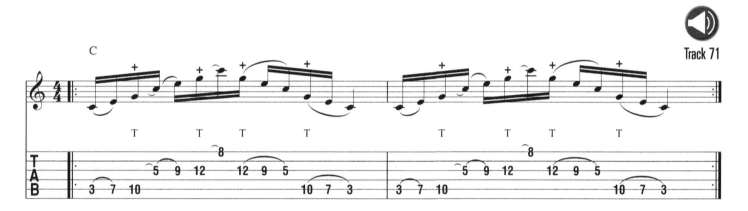

Here's the minor variation on the previous example. In this example, the same three-note arpeggio (D–F–A) is used on strings 5, 3, and 1. You use a different right-hand finger to tap on each different string. This is a cool one!

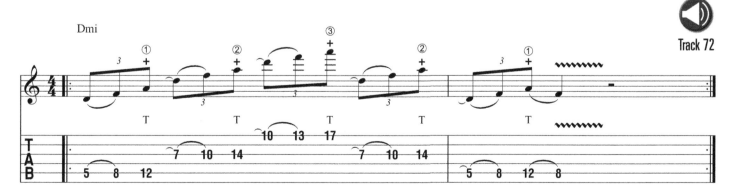

In this example, we're pairing two left-hand hammered notes with one tapped note to sound the root, ♭7th, and 3rd of a dominant 7th chord. We alternate between the forms built on the sixth string and fifth string to outline a cycle of fifths progression.

Track 73

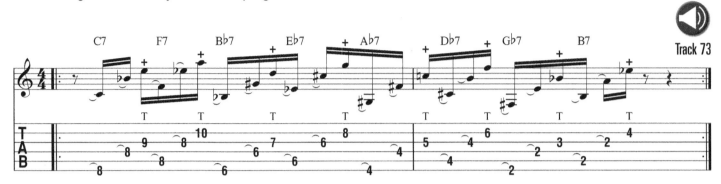

This example uses a tapped F pedal tone above C, B♭, and B chords hammered by the left hand. The three-over-four syncopation is a nice effect.

Track 74

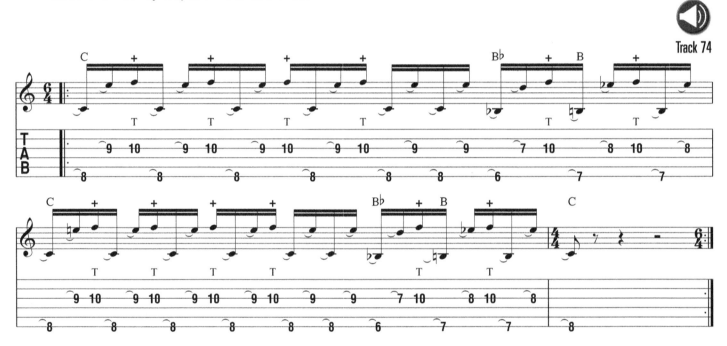

This last example, an E minor Latin groove, is using the tapping technique as a slap percussion sound. While the left hand hammers out a syncopated bass line, the right hand is used to provide rhythmic accents throughout. The chordal accents on the 'and' of beat 3 should be plucked with your right hand.

SP = Slap percussion with the middle and ring fingers of the right hand.
USP = Up slap percussion with the index and ring fingers of the right hand.

Track 75

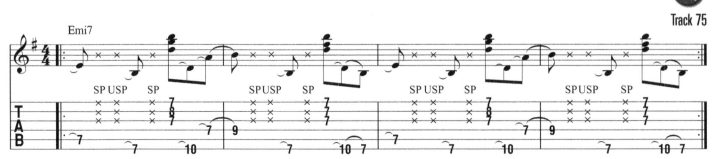

Acknowledgments

Thanks to:

All at Hal Leonard Corporation.
Alex Grunge for engineering, producing, and editing.
Ernst Homeyer for the fastest transcriptions ever!
Marie-Christine Belkadi for maintaining my website:
www.home.earthlink.net/~mcb1
Beth Marlis from Musicians Institute at www.mi.edu
Nick Roubas for his Nick Roubas guitar at violuthier.com
Joe Iacobellis at everlymusic.com for his strings.
Steve Blutcher at DiMarzio.com
Koa Truong, Ernst Homeyer, and Alain Lasseube for their knowledge and friendship.

This book is dedicated to my brother and top French guitarist Alain Lasseube.

About the Author

Jean Marc Belkadi started playing guitar at age 14. He graduated from the Toulhouse Music Conservatory in his hometown. In 1984, he left France for the U.S. to study at Musicians Institute in Hollywood where he received the Best Guitarist of the Year award.

In 1989 and 1992, he was awarded third and second prize at the Billboard Song Contest. For three years, he was musical director of the Johnny Hune TV show. He has written six guitar method books and CDs: *A Modern Approach to Jazz, Rock & Fusion Guitar, Advanced Scale Concepts and Licks for Guitar, Jazz-Rock Triad Improvising for Guitar, Slap and Pop Technique for Guitar, The Diminished Scale for Guitar,* and *Outside Licks for Guitar.*

He has recorded one solo album and teaches at the Musicians Institute of Technology in Hollywood.

MUSICIANS INSTITUTE PRESS is the official series of Southern California's renowned music school, Musicians Institute. MI instructors, some of the finest musicians in the world, share their vast knowledge and experience with you – no matter what your current level. For guitar, bass, drums, vocals, and keyboards, MI Press offers the finest music curriculum for higher learning through a variety of series:

ESSENTIAL CONCEPTS	**MASTER CLASS**	**PRIVATE LESSONS**
Designed from MI core curriculum programs.	*Designed from MI elective courses.*	*Tackle a variety of topics "one-on one" with MI faculty instructors.*

GUITAR

Acoustic Artistry
by Evan Hirschelman • **Private Lessons**
00695922 Book/Online Audio $24.99

Advanced Scale Concepts & Licks for Guitar
by Jean Marc Belkadi • **Private Lessons**
00695298 Book/CD Pack $22.99

All-in-One Guitar Soloing Course
by Daniel Gilbert & Beth Marlis
00217709 Book/Online Media $29.99

Blues/Rock Soloing for Guitar
by Robert Calva • **Private Lessons**
00695680 Book/Online Audio $22.99

Blues Guitar Soloing
by Keith Wyatt • **Master Class**
00695132 Book/Online Audio $29.99

Blues Rhythm Guitar
by Keith Wyatt • **Master Class**
00695131 Book/Online Audio $22.99

Dean Brown
00696002 DVD $29.95

Chord Progressions for Guitar
by Tom Kolb • **Private Lessons**
00695664 Book/Online Audio $19.99

Chord Tone Soloing
by Barrett Tagliarino • **Private Lessons**
00695855 Book/Online Audio $27.99

Chord-Melody Guitar
by Bruce Buckingham • **Private Lessons**
00695646 Book/Online Audio $22.99

Classical & Fingerstyle Guitar Techniques
by David Oakes • **Master Class**
00695171 Book/Online Audio $22.99

Classical Themes for Electric Guitar
by Jean Marc Belkadi • **Private Lessons**
00695806 Book/CD Pack $15.99

Country Guitar
by Al Bonhomme • **Master Class**
00695661 Book/Online Audio $22.99

Essential Rhythm Guitar
by Steve Trovato • **Private Lessons**
00695181 Book/CD Pack $16.99

Exotic Scales & Licks for Electric Guitar
by Jean Marc Belkadi • **Private Lessons**
00695860 Book/CD Pack $19.99

Funk Guitar
by Ross Bolton • **Private Lessons**
00695419 Book/Online Audio $17.99

Guitar Basics
by Bruce Buckingham • **Private Lessons**
00695134 Book/Online Audio $19.99

Guitar Fretboard Workbook
by Barrett Tagliarino • **Essential Concepts**
00695712 . . . . $22.99

Guitar Hanon
by Peter Deneff • **Private Lessons**
00695321 . . . . $17.99

Guitar Lick•tionary
by Dave Hill • **Private Lessons**
00695482 Book/CD Pack $22.99

Guitar Soloing
by Dan Gilbert & Beth Marlis • **Essential Concepts**
00695190 Book/Online Audio $24.99

Harmonics
by Jamie Findlay • **Private Lessons**
00695169 Book/CD Pack $16.99

Harmony & Theory
by Keith Wyatt & Carl Schroeder • **Essential Concepts**
00695161 . . . . $24.99

Introduction to Jazz Guitar Soloing
by Joe Elliott • **Master Class**
00695406 Book/Online Audio $24.99

Jazz Guitar Chord System
by Scott Henderson • **Private Lessons**
00695291 . . . . $14.99

Jazz Guitar Improvisation
by Sid Jacobs • **Master Class**
00217711 Book/Online Media $19.99

Jazz, Rock & Funk Guitar
by Dean Brown • **Private Lessons**
00217690 Book/Online Media $19.99

Latin Guitar
by Bruce Buckingham • **Master Class**
00695379 Book/Online Audio $19.99

Lead Sheet Bible
by Robin Randall & Janice Peterson • **Private Lessons**
00695130 Book/Online Audio $24.99

Liquid Legato
by Allen Hinds • **Private Lessons**
00696656 Book/Online Audio $17.99

Modern Jazz Concepts for Guitar
by Sid Jacobs • **Master Class**
00695711 Book/CD Pack $19.99

Modern Rock Rhythm Guitar
by Danny Gill • **Private Lessons**
00695682 Book/Online Audio $22.99

Modes for Guitar
by Tom Kolb • **Private Lessons**
00695555 Book/Online Audio $19.99

Music Reading for Guitar
by David Oakes • **Essential Concepts**
00695192 . . . . $24.99

Outside Guitar Licks
by Jean Marc Belkadi • **Private Lessons**
00695697 Book/CD Pack $16.99

Power Plucking
by Dale Turner • **Private Lesson**
00695962 Book/CD Pack $19.95

Progressive Tapping Licks
by Jean Marc Belkadi • **Private Lessons**
00695748 Book/CD Pack $19.99

Rhythm Guitar
by Bruce Buckingham & Eric Paschal • **Essential Concepts**
00695188 Book $22.99
00114559 Book/Online Audio $27.99
00695909 DVD $19.95

Rhythmic Lead Guitar
by Barrett Tagliarino • **Private Lessons**
00110263 Book/Online Audio $22.99

Rock Lead Basics
by Nick Nolan & Danny Gill • **Master Class**
00695144 Book/Online Audio $19.99

Rock Lead Performance
by Nick Nolan & Danny Gill • **Master Class**
00695278 Book/Online Audio $19.99

Rock Lead Techniques
by Nick Nolan & Danny Gill • **Master Class**
00695146 Book/Online Audio $19.99

Shred Guitar
by Greg Harrison • **Master Class**
00695977 Book/Online Audio $24.99

Solo Slap Guitar
by Jude Gold • **Master Class**
00139556 Book/Online Video $24.99

Technique Exercises for Guitar
by Jean Marc Belkadi • **Private Lessons**
00695913 Book/CD Pack $17.99

Texas Blues Guitar
by Robert Calva • **Private Lessons**
00695340 Book/Online Audio $19.99

Ultimate Guitar Technique
by Bill LaFleur • **Private Lessons**
00695863 Book/Online Audio $24.99

Prices, contents, and availability subject to change without notice.

HAL•LEONARD®
7777 W. BLUEMOUND RD. P.O. BOX 13819 MILWAUKEE, WI 53213

www.halleonard.com